# BITTERNESS

# BITTERNESS

ROBERT S. MCGEE
AND
PAT SPRINGLE

Rapha Publishing/Word, Inc.
Houston and Dallas, TX

**Bitterness**
by Robert S. McGee and Pat Springle


First Printing, 1991
ISBN: 0-945276-38-9
Printed in the United States of America

# *Contents*

# *How Does Bitterness Develop?*

Bitterness is anger that has been repressed and has festered. Over weeks, months, and years, anger from unforgiven wounds and injustices simmers in its own venom, increasing until it consumes the angry person.

Christians speak often of forgiveness and love; but ironically, they sometimes have a difficult time applying those biblical truths to their own anger and hatred. In too many Sunday school classes and other church groups, well-meaning leaders condemn all feelings of anger as sin. They imply that only "bad Christians" feel anger. Few Christians can stand the threat of being labeled—by themselves or others—as "bad"; their identities are too wrapped up in being "good." So they practice denial, trying to convince themselves that their anger and hatred isn't really anger and hatred at all. "I'm just *frustrated*," they claim. Meanwhile, the repression continues and the anger builds. They explode from time to time and then feel ashamed of themselves, doing penance by feeling bad enough long enough to pay for the terrible sin of exploding in anger. But they fail to find a true biblical solution, one that encompasses the causes of their emotions and differentiates between feeling angry and taking revenge. As a result, they fail to begin the process of healing that can help them actually experience Paul's admonishment to the believers at Ephesus: "Be angry, and yet do not sin; do not let the sun go down on your anger, and do not give the devil an opportunity" (Ephesians 4:26–27).

Once, a friend of mine accidentally cut his hand with a knife. Instead of accepting the compassion and help of those around him, he became tense and angry toward everyone. While motioning violently with his other hand, he glared at them and yelled, "Get back! Get away from me!" Later, he asked me, "Why would getting hurt produce such violence? There must be a lot of anger buried somewhere in me. In fact, I guess you could call it rage. I was really out of control." It's natural for people to protect themselves against being hurt. Similarly, anger about being hurt is a natural, reflexive response, a defense reaction that may also be coupled with self-imposed isolation. When this response occurs, angry persons push others away, telling even friends and loved ones to "Get back!" Then the love and compassion they genuinely crave are overridden by defense mechanisms they believe will keep them from being hurt. As a result, they remain isolated and unconsoled, even when they need love most, and their anger festers into bitterness.

Some people remind us of ourselves. We may project our problems onto them, and we may even hate them for their similarities to us. Other people remind us of those who have hurt us deeply. In our minds, we transfer the characteristics of the hurtful person to the new person. For instance, if someone reminds me of my first employer, my instinctive response is to feel the same toward him as I did toward that employer.

## Hating Ourselves

Sometimes people feel hatred toward themselves. In some families, expressing anger at parents or siblings brings quick condemnation. Members of those families learn to focus their anger on themselves instead of their parents or siblings. The result can be damaging to one's self-image.

Recently I led a group on the subject of anger and asked, "What kind of names do you call yourself?"

"Stupid," one gentleman said. A lady said she called herself "fat moron," though she was very attractive and obviously bright. Other responses were "dumb nerd," "jerk," and "scumball." When one person said, "I really can't tell this group. It's a little too crude," lots of other people nodded and laughed nervously.

I asked, "Do any of you call yourselves names like, 'smart,' 'beautiful,' 'handsome,' 'loved,' 'valuable,' or anything like that?"

A short, bald man in the back said, "Yeah, but I don't believe it!"

Everybody laughed again.

"If you heard a person calling someone else the names you call yourself, what conclusions would you come to? How would that person seem to feel about the other?"

Several people looked reflective; then a lady said, "I'd say the first one hates the other—*really hates* that person."

Many people call themselves degrading, derogatory names as punishment for the slightest mistakes. They take revenge on themselves by attacking or blaming themselves, or by withholding something they need. This condemnation often arises from implicit conclusions they drew long ago that they are bad, shameful people, unworthy of love, and fully deserving of all the pain they can inflict upon themselves . . . and probably much more. This continual condemnation can easily evolve into bitterness.

## Hating Others

Feelings of hurt and anger toward others often remain locked away due to blind loyalty, refusal to betray the "family secret," expected reprisals, or fear of the power these emotions would have if they were expressed.

As angry, hurting persons experience healing, they become increasingly objective about themselves and their families. They begin to feel the emotions they have repressed so long. They risk being honest (if only a little bit!) with those who help them feel safe, and the healing process continues.

Typically, people in denial protect and defend those who have hurt them. One woman who had been physically abused by her father and brother said, "I love them, and I know they love me. They just didn't know how to express it."

As she continued going to a group and listening to others, she began to see what love really is . . . and what it isn't. For several weeks, she sat in the group, quiet and confused. As realization slowly dawned on her, she entered a state of shock. "I can't believe it. I just can't believe it," she said over and over. A couple of months later, the group's nurturing environment had provided enough safety and strength for her repressed hatred to surface. One night she exploded. "I'd like to kill both of them for what they did to me!" she cried. As soon as she said it, she was overwhelmed with shame for having expressed what she truly felt. She then returned to emotional hiding. It took three more months before she could talk openly again in the group about her feelings toward her father and brother.

This woman's response was typical of those who finally come to grips with injustice that has been inflicted on them. A common sequence of responses is denial, initial realization, shock, explosions, shame, then more progress. After a while, people in this process cease to be surprised when more repressed hurt and anger are uncovered. "I'm not that surprised anymore," a friend admitted. "I used to be shocked every time I saw more of it, but I guess I'm more comfortable with the reality of the *depth* of my wounds. I don't expect quick cures like I did at first. We talk about 'the process,' and that's exactly what it is, a process of feeling and forgiving."

In the early stages of the healing process, most people become aware of the damage inflicted on them primarily by one or two people—for instance, a parent who was sexually abusive or who smothered the child with control. As the healing process continues, however, more intense anger may be revealed toward another person in the family, typically the other parent, who failed to protect the child from harm.

Describing her verbally abusive, controlling mother, Alicia said, "I couldn't even pick out which clothes to wear to school.

Mother told me what to wear, who to spend time with, and even what to say to them. Every day she quizzed me about each conversation I'd had, and if I hadn't guessed what she wanted me to say, boy, she let me have it! I didn't have a life of my own."

"Tell me about your dad," I said.

"Oh, Dad was great. He never did all that kind of stuff to me. He spent most of his time in the den reading. He couldn't stand her, either!" she laughed.

"Did he ever stop your mother from controlling or criticizing you?"

"Well . . . no, not really. Sometimes he'd hear me crying in my room and come to tell me he understood. I appreciated that."

Alicia had trouble being objective about her mother because she believed her mother's control was the same as love. Slowly, however, she realized that love is not manipulative, smothering, and condemning. That's when Alicia started making real progress. Much later, however, as she grieved and learned to forgive her mother, Alicia's focus shifted to her father.

"All these years I felt so positive about my dad. I guess that's because he was nicer to me than Mother was. But now I realize that he could have done *a lot more* than hide in the den and sneak upstairs to my room to console me a little. He could have stopped her! He could have been the man in the family and stood up to her! But he didn't. He's a wimp . . . a real wimp. He—just as much as Mother—robbed me of a happy childhood. Mother inflicted the wounds, and he just stood by and watched."

Repressed hatred—hatred she had no idea even existed—surfaced, and Alicia continued the painful process of grieving, forgiving, and taking responsibility for her healing process.

## Rage

Some people keep the clamps on their anger and hatred because they are only too aware of the monster of furious rage that boils within them. When that monster breaks its bonds and explodes—which seldom occurs if they have strong control or often occurs if their control is weakened by added stresses—these people change from Jekyll to Hyde, from numb to passionate, from passive to violent.

"I don't know what happens to me," related Dorothy, confused and depressed. "Most of the time I'm a good wife and a good mother. I really love my children, but sometimes . . . something snaps . . . . Maybe the two-year-old has spilled something again—usually that's okay, but sometimes . . . . My stepson didn't come home last Thursday night and Jim [her husband] didn't even care. I woke him up several times in the night to tell him. I didn't sleep a wink—*but he didn't care!* I sat in the bed looking at him. I wanted to hit him so bad! Finally, I . . . I started screaming at him. I wouldn't stop for a long time, and every time he tried to calm me down, I just got madder."

Some people may feel intense hatred toward someone for hurting them (although they may only admit to being "a little bothered" or "frustrated"), but if the threat of expressing their rage toward that person is too great, they displace their anger. One man from a verbally abusive family played sports to "let out some tension," but the competition only reminded him that he couldn't measure up in the eyes of his parents. When he won, he felt superior and arrogant, but when he lost, he violently bashed lockers and trash cans, then wildly sped off in his car. His case demonstrates that attempts to control rage may be successful in the short-run, but tighter clamps ultimately cause more repression, shame, and denial. This repression leads to a greater reservoir of hatred that will eventually explode in rage.

Many people turn to "pain killers" such as alcohol, drugs, work, food, power, or anything else that promises to cover up the pain of repressed anger. Like other attempts to control anger, these choices also tighten the clamps, creating more pressure, and ironically, assuring more or bigger explosions of uncontrolled rage.

## Hating God

For many people, the ultimate threat is admitting that they hate God for letting them suffer abuse, humiliation, and emptiness. Their attitude toward Him may be very similar to their attitude toward a parent who failed to protect them. They may not be aware of their anger at God until they are well into the healing process; then their disappointment may be similar to Asaph's as described in Psalm 77. He turned to the Lord for help, but was not comforted.

> In the day of my trouble I sought the Lord;
> In the night my hand was stretched out without weariness;
> My soul refused to be comforted.
> When I remember God, then I am disturbed;
> When I sigh, then my spirit grows faint.
> Thou hast held my eyelids open;
> I am so troubled that I cannot speak.
>
> Psalm 77:2–4

Later, the psalmist reflected on the seeming hopelessness of trusting in God, questioning God's goodness and purposes in his life:

Will the Lord reject forever?
And will He never be favorable again?
Has His lovingkindness ceased forever?
Has His promise come to an end forever?
Has God forgotten to be gracious?
Or has He in anger withdrawn His compassion?

Psalm 77:7–9

Many people feel that God can't be trusted, that He has let them down. They are disappointed in God, and that disappointment is only a short step from blaming Him for their hurt or for not protecting them from being wounded. And that disappointment and blame are only another short step from hate.

"It scares me to even say it," Joseph said cautiously, "but if I'm really honest, I have to admit that I hate God. If He is so powerful and loving, why did He let my parents divorce? Why did He let my dad have a heart attack? Why didn't God cause my folks to love each other . . . and love me? I'm afraid to feel all the rage that I have kept bottled up inside. I'm afraid a bolt of lightning will strike me."

In his book, *Disappointment with God*, (Zondervan: Grand Rapids, MI, 1988) Philip Yancey describes the necessity of being honest *about* God, as well as *with* God. Grieving one's losses includes not only those losses created and allowed by people, but those allowed by God, too. Fear of God's authority may complicate this process, but a patient and wise group leader, friend, or counselor can help sort out the complexities so *all* hurts can be grieved.

## The Power of Bitterness

Love transforms. So does bitterness. Love stimulates creativity and freshness of thought; it energizes people to care for others and brings affirmation and freedom. Love builds.

In contrast, bitterness destroys. It sucks the freshness out of life and focuses attention and efforts on "getting even" and hurting others.

Anger's initial motive may be justice. But rather than seeking a just solution that is ultimately constructive, hatred seeks to wound, hurt, humiliate, and destroy. And it is very successful when expressed through verbal and nonverbal condemnation, sarcasm and outright ridicule, attacks and abandonment, and aggressive, passive, and passive-aggressive means.

Jealousy of others' successes is only a half-step away from hatred. When people compare themselves to others and thus perceive themselves as deficient, the resulting anger can easily turn into hatred—and a desire to hurt the one who has "shown them up."

But in their passion to hurt others, those who lash out in bitterness hurt themselves, too. At the least, they waste precious time on negative, harmful exercises. Usually, though, the tragedy of hatred is much more costly. It consumes people with a passion for revenge that may eventually cause depression or various psychosomatic illnesses.

Admitting hatred is a big step, but it is only one step toward genuine, emotional health. Though they need to keep growing, some people get stuck after this admission.

# *Choosing to Forgive*

Forgiveness—releasing someone from a debt—is a central issue in life. When someone hurts another person, a debt is incurred. A sense of justice cries out, *He owes me!* Love and justice are the cornerstones of emotional stability. Writing about a child's innate sense of love and justice, author and theologian John Stott says:

> Justice without mercy is too strict, and mercy without justice too lenient . . . , children know this instinctively . . . . The

> two most poignant cries of a child are 'Nobody loves me' and 'It isn't fair.' Their sense of love and justice comes from God, who made them in His image, and who revealed Himself as holy love at the cross.[1]

Forgiveness doesn't come naturally. It seems awkward, at best; to some it seems absurd. In his article about forgiveness, "An Unnatural Act," Philip Yancey observes that all the laws of nature and economics are based on attitudes of eat or be eaten and take what you can get.[2] But he outlines three compelling motivations to go against the grain and forgive the offender. These reasons are "breaking the cycle of blame and pain," "loosening the stronghold of guilt on us and others," and

1 John R. W. Stott. *The Cross of Christ*, IVP: Downers Grove, IL, 1986, p. 297.

2 Philip Yancey, "An Unnatural Act," *Christianity Today*, April 8, 1991, pp. 36–39.

"helping us understand that we are just like others—all of us need forgiveness."

The cleansing refreshment of genuine forgiveness is attractive, but sadly alien, to many people.

## Two Errors

Christians (and nonbelievers alike) tend to make one of two errors: They either forgive too quickly or not at all. Many conscientious Christians can quote Scripture about forgiveness. They know they *should* forgive—and they feel terribly ashamed when they don't! So they go through the motions of doing it. But something's wrong. When Christians talk about the wounds in their lives, they inevitably talk about a parent or a spouse who has hurt them deeply. Inevitably, their response is like that of a pastor I talked with. When I mentioned a childhood problem he had endured because of his father, he interrupted me.

" . . . but I've already forgiven him for that!" the pastor insisted, although he had ceased to function normally because of his repressed anger toward his father. These turbulent, unexpressed feelings had pushed him into clinical depression.

"Do you think there may be some hurts you haven't grieved about yet?" I asked.

He looked at me resentfully. "I told you. I've already forgiven him!"

Forgiveness is the release from a debt—the *whole* debt, not just part of it. Devout, well-intentioned Christians sometimes forgive as soon as they become aware of pain; but often, their compulsion to forgive quickly short circuits the process of grieving the real wound and forgiving the real offense.

Incomplete forgiveness produces repressed hurt and anger, but it also produces considerable confusion. "After all," the injured person insists, "I have done all I know to do. I forgave, didn't I?" So why do the feelings of hurt and anger continue? In their confusion, people repress these feelings and depression often results. Then hopelessness is added to the problems of compulsive forgiving, hurt, anger, and confusion.

As the pastor mentioned earlier began to understand his incomplete forgiveness of his father, his defensive resentment slowly faded. "So that's why I'm still depressed," he said. "I *thought* I had forgiven him, but . . . yeah, I'm hurting a lot more than I care to admit. I'm scared of it. And I'm so embarrassed! After all, I'm a pastor! I'm not *supposed* to be depressed."

On the other end of the spectrum are those who refuse to forgive at all. "Never!" one woman screamed. "I'll never forgive him for what he did to me!" The woman had been wounded by her verbally abusive husband, but her deepest wounds were caused by his physical abuse of their children. "And what he did to Billy and Lee Ann . . . . Only an animal would treat children that way!"

Both incomplete forgiveness and no forgiveness lead to more bitterness. People who hold on to their bitterness usually find that the deep, festering wounds of the past are compounded by daily interaction with other people. Bitter people look for faults to blame, not love to nurture.

The ability to forgive is tied to the personal experience of Christ's forgiveness (Colossians 3:13). To put it another way, we will be unable to truly forgive others for their sins toward us if we don't experience forgiveness for our own sins toward God and others.

This realization is a turning point. Many people have repressed their hurt for years. They've been afraid of the rage they have glimpsed in themselves from time to time, and they have sensed an overwhelming emptiness and hopelessness lurking in the recesses of their hearts. They have been wounded. They have been wronged. They are victims.

This "victim mentality" can become so pervasive that the "victims" don't assume responsibility for their own sinful behavior. They are victims, but they are also victimizers. For example, in a heated exchange between spouses during a counseling session, the wife continuously blamed the husband for the couple's problems. I waited for a lull in the fight, then asked, "Cindy, you have listed things James has done wrong . . . things he is responsible for. What are some things *you* have done wrong in the relationship?"

She looked stunned, then angry. "Why ask *me* a question like that? *He's* the one who hurt *me*! I haven't done anything *close* to what he's done to me!"

This kind of blame-shifting is black or white, all or nothing. Cindy's bitterness continued to fester because she was unwilling to admit that she had been wrong, too.

According to her, all of their problems were her husband's fault. To be sure, some of them were! But forgiveness, reconciliation, intimacy, respect, and even communication were blocked because Cindy was unwilling to be honest about her own sins in the relationship.

Another marital conversation started out in a similar way with both partners blaming each other and defending themselves. But after a while, the husband said, "I blew it. I was wrong when I . . . . " His admission of fault and responsibility didn't solve all their problems right away, but it did open the door so that solutions could be found.

While some people try to bury their own sinfulness by blaming someone else, others go to the opposite extreme. They assume that *everything* is their fault. When these people take the first steps in the healing process and become aware of the magnitude of the hurt and anger in their lives, they often flip-flop, assigning all the blame to the offenders. Wise friends and counselors can help them sort out what is *their* responsibility and what is *others'* responsibility, what they need to confess and what they need to grieve.

Confessing sins toward God and others takes courage, but it frees people from the cycles of repression and blame. This is not just a modern-day experience. King David long ago described his silence and unwillingness to take responsibility for his sin in terms that indicate that his silence led to depression:

> When I kept silent about my sin,
> my body wasted away
> Through my groaning all day long.
> For day and night
> Thy hand was heavy upon me;
> My vitality was drained away
> as with the fever heat of summer.
>
> Psalm 32:3–4

Admitting his wrongs, however, brought David both physical and emotional refreshment:

> I acknowledged my sin to Thee,
> And my iniquity I did not hide;
> I said, "I will confess
> my transgression to the Lord";
> And Thou didst forgive
> the guilt of my sin.
>
> Thou art my hiding place;
> Thou dost preserve me from
> trouble;
> Thou dost surround me with songs
> of deliverance.
>
> Psalm 32:5, 7

Forgiveness means releasing others from the debt of the wounds they have inflicted. It creates a renewed opportunity to base relationships on integrity and mutual respect.

If others can accept forgiveness, solid, lasting relationships can be built. If others continue to blame or control, they can still be forgiven, but their actions will hinder their relationships.

Joseph's life clearly illustrates forgiveness and restitution based on trust which was tested and found true. Joseph's brothers wanted to kill him, but instead, they sold him into slavery in Egypt. After being falsely accused of adultery, Joseph languished in a dungeon for many years. The Lord enabled Joseph to interpret the Pharaoh's dreams, and Joseph was then made prime minister of Egypt, second only to Pharaoh.

A severe famine devastated the land, just as Joseph had predicted, and his brothers came to Egypt looking for food, unaware that Joseph had been made prime minister. Before revealing his identity, Joseph tested his brothers to see if they would again forsake a brother as they had forsaken him. He secretly hid silver in their bags, caught them, and accused them of thievery. He insisted that they leave Jacob's youngest son, Benjamin, as a hostage. After a long series of stern tests, Joseph was satisfied that he could trust his repentant brothers. He revealed his true identity as their brother, forgave them, and restored his relationship with them.

In the same way, the sincerity of those who have been hurtful and controlling in the past can be "tested" to see if they are sincerely willing to have relationships based on trust and respect. Patience and honesty can provide a foundation for trust to grow.

Forgiveness does not necessitate restitution. It provides a platform to develop a relationship if both parties are willing. Many people will insist on having relationships only on *their* terms. Their onslaught of manipulation (including accusations of *others'* selfish behavior) can cause people to revert to their subservient positions of being controlled again. Such relationships should be refused. However, the option to build a relationship established on respect and honesty can be offered.

Sometimes a person feels he or she cannot forgive someone else for a past offense. There are many ways a person can try to justify unforgiveness.

## Reasons for Unforgiveness

People often fail to forgive others (and themselves) because they don't think it's possible. They forget that God has graciously forgiven all His children's sins through Christ's death, and they rationalize why they can't forgive. The following excuses are some of the ways people rationalize their unwillingness to forgive themselves and others:

- ***The offense was too great.*** Grant's wife had left him for another man, and he was bitter toward her. Her infidelity was too great a sin for him to forgive. But almost two years after the incident, God began to impress Grant with the idea that he should forgive his wife, *just as God in Christ also had forgiven (him)*, completely and willfully. When Grant finally did forgive her, he felt as though 100 pounds had been lifted from his back.

Roger sat shaking with anger as he recalled his wife's rape. His anger was destroying his health and his relationship with his wife. *How can any man, who really is a man, forgive such an act?* he wondered. The transient who had raped his wife had moved on, and in his perversion, had probably forgotten the incident. He was never caught. Continuing to allow the offense to produce bitterness might ultimately do more harm to Roger and his family than the destructive act of the rape.

- ***He(she) won't accept responsibility for the offense.*** How many people have offended us, but won't agree that they were at fault? The offense might be something slight, such as being overlooked at a social event, or something major, such as being emotionally neglected as a child. Having others agree that they've offended us isn't necessary for us to respond properly to their offense.

- ***He(she) isn't truly sorry.*** John pulled a practical joke on you which caused you to be late for class, and your professor refused to accept your paper because you didn't have it in on time. John doesn't see anything wrong with a little joke—he's slightly sorry, but he still thinks it was hilarious. Even if John doesn't recognize the trouble he's caused you, you can still extend forgiveness to him through Christ, and refuse to hold the offense against him.

- ***He(she) never asked to be forgiven.*** For whatever reason, the offender never got around to asking you for forgiveness. Are you going to withhold forgiveness until it's requested? Who is suffering, you or the offender? What would God have you do? (Read 1 Corinthians 13:5 and Ephesians 4:32.)

- ***He(she) will do it again.*** Candy's husband had been out late playing cards on every Friday night for three years. On some nights, he didn't come home. "Me? Forgive that jerk?" Candy asked. The Lord said that the number of times we're to forgive is seventy times seven . . . in other words, regardless of the number of offenses. If Candy doesn't forgive, she will be the bitter loser.

- ***He(she) did it again.*** David had been a horrible husband to Mandy. However, after much effort, Mandy had forgiven him for his insensitivity, his greater concern for the guys on his softball team, his lack of affection for the children, and his callous, domineering attitude. Then, David saw how poor his behavior had become. He began to change. His relationship with Mandy started to improve—until he stayed out late again with the guys. He had done it again! One mistake set the whole conflict in motion again.

- ***I don't like him(her).*** Generally, we don't have a great deal of appreciation for those who have wronged us. In fact, every emotion within us may call for retaliation against the creep! Only when we realize that forgiveness is an act of the will, and not of the emotions, will we choose to forgive those who have hurt us.

- ***He(she) did it deliberately.*** "He knew what he was doing, and he did it anyway." George had been swindled out of $10,000 by his "best friend," Hal. It had been a complex scheme which had required precise timing over a period of several months. As George sat stunned, his mind raced through those times he had been generous to Hal. He thought of how much he had loved Hal and had repeatedly trusted him. The swindle had been completely deliberate, and Hal had used him. George had been played for a sucker. Hal must be laughing at him now. Whether the offense was deliberate or not, God still wants George to forgive Hal.

• ***If I forgive the offense, I'll have to treat the offender well.*** Ben excused his slander of Steve by pointing out how Steve had offended him. He felt justified in destroying Steve's reputation even though most of the things he had said about Steve were lies.

Shirley was cold to Greg, and had been for two weeks. It was her plan to punish him for two weeks because he had offended her. She would forgive him all right—as soon as she was through punishing him.

- ***Someone has to punish him(her).*** How often do we want God to be merciful to us and yet want Him to skin other people alive? When we don't see them suffer, we sometimes take it upon ourselves to be God's hand of vengeance.

Charles was their pastor, but according to Gloria, he had wasted the church's money. Gloria was in charge of the church women's group. She waited patiently for God to nail Charles, but when God didn't do what she thought He should, she just knew that she was to be the divining rod for Charlie's back. Soon the church had taken sides—pro-Charles or anti-Charles. The result was that the church disgraced itself by splitting in hatred.

Discipline is God's job. *Vengeance is Mine, I will repay,* says the Lord . . . and

He hasn't delegated that responsibility to us!

- ***Something keeps me from forgiving.*** Satan actively promotes unforgiveness. When you attempt to deal with this problem honestly, you may be in for a tremendous spiritual battle, with both confusing and conflicting thoughts and emotions. Don't be surprised if you have to resist Satan at every turn in order to accomplish the task of forgiving the offender. Forgiveness is primarily an act of the will, not a warm feeling.

- ***I'll be a hypocrite if I forgive, because I don't feel like forgiving.*** It's amazing how we confuse hypocrisy with obedience. We are hypocritical only if we do something for selfish gain. For instance, a hypocrite might be a politician who comes to church in order to get its members to vote for him in the next election, but who despises the church and its people. To forgive as an act of the will in obedience to the Lord's command is true spirituality, not hypocrisy.

- ***I'll forgive, but I won't ever forget.*** If we continue to harbor the memory of an offense, we are only fooling ourselves in thinking that we have forgiven the offender, and we will not experience any freedom. In true forgiveness, we give up the right to remember an offense or to bring it up again during arguments. (Note: This doesn't mean that when we forgive a wrong, we'll *never* think of it again. But it does mean that we won't relish the memory. Choose to think about things that are true, honorable, right, pure, and lovely [Philippians 4:8].)

- ***I'll forgive, because I have found an excuse for the offense.*** Hank had been very irresponsible during the early years of his marriage. His wife, Sally, had always been able to forgive him by placing the blame on his mother, who had babied Hank even after he was grown. And yet, Sally was continually angered by Hank and his mother. In fact, her volatile temper was destroying her marriage.

Sally thought that she had forgiven Hank when she had really just excused him. By blaming Hank's mother for his immaturity, she had rationalized his behavior, and had reduced her perception of his offensive actions like this:

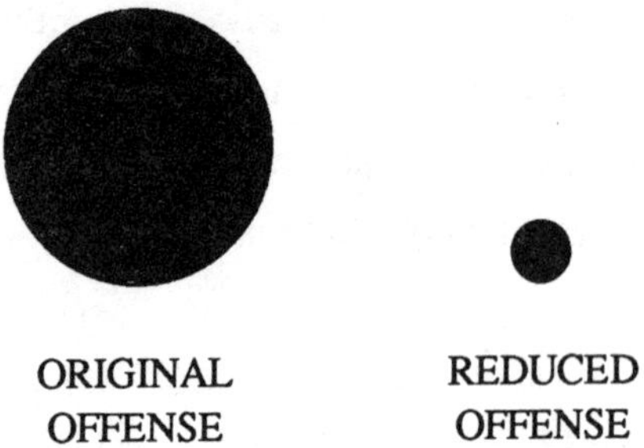


After reducing each offense, Sally then forgave it. The problem was that she did not deal with the real offense, but with a distortion of it. Therefore, the real offense remained intact in spite of her efforts at "forgiveness."

When you offend someone, or when someone offends you, do you immediately look for a "reason"? If you do, you may only be rationalizing. If you come up with an excuse to the question, *Why did I forgive him (or her)?* then you have not truly forgiven the offense. You have excused it.

## Results of Unforgiveness

- ***Stress***: Sarah announced to the group that her husband did not deserve to be forgiven, and that she wasn't going to forgive him if it meant her life. It did. Sarah died of kidney failure. She wanted to kill her husband, but in reality she killed herself. Countless people live under extreme stress due to the bitterness and anger that result from unforgiveness.

- ***Self-Inflicted Reinjury:*** Robert recalled this incident: "As I drove home, flashing into my memory was a guy I played basketball with in college. He was a great antagonist of mine. He was one of the few people I have ever met whom I truly wanted to punch out. I began to remember the unkind things he did to me. Soon, anger started creeping up inside of me. I had not remembered this fellow for years, and I'm sure that he doesn't remember me at all. Yet, my reliving this event caused me a lot of pain. I had not properly dealt with it in the beginning."

  How many times are you reinjuring yourself because past offenses haunt you?

- ***No More Love:*** "I don't know if I can ever love someone again" is a frequent complaint from those offended by a lover. Our deepest hurts come from those we love. One way we deal with the pain of being offended is to simply withdraw, refusing to love anymore. We often make this unconscious decision when we have not adequately dealt with an offense. We may desperately want to love again, but feel that we are incapable of it. Refusing to experience love and feeling unable to love are both devastating conditions.

- ***Bitterness:*** Emotions trace their lines on our faces. We think others don't notice what's going on inside, but our anger can usually be detected by even the casual observer. One person recalled seeing a neighbor go through difficulties in her marriage. Hate created such an impression on her that her face became permanently snarled. She still has that ugly look on her face. Unforgiveness produces ugliness of all sorts.

- ***Perpetual Conflict:*** A couple, both of whom had been previously married, received counseling several years ago. Having been hurt in their first marriage, they each anticipated hurt from their present spouse. At the smallest offense, they would each react as if their spouse were about to deliver the final blow. They were constantly on the defensive, protecting themselves from the attacks they imagined their mate would deliver. Having been offended in the past, they anticipated more hurt in the present and future, and reacted in a way that perpetuated the conflict.

- ***Walls That Keep Others Out:*** Strangely, many of us refuse to experience love from those who love us. We may often become anxious and threatened when personal intimacy becomes possible.

  Jane hoped and prayed that her husband Frank would come to know the Lord. This, she thought, would enable him to be more loving toward her and their children. One day, Frank accepted Christ and over time, his life began to change. He became interested in Jane, and started spending time with her and the children. He was sensitive and loving. Was it a dream come true? Instead of rejoicing, Jane deeply resented Frank for not changing sooner! *If Frank is able to love us like this now, then he's always had the ability,* she thought. She felt confused and guilty about her anger.

Jane's anger was a defense mechanism to keep distance between Frank and herself. The closer that they might get, the more pain she might experience if he reverted to his old ways. She had never truly forgiven Frank, so the bricks of unforgiveness were stacked to form a wall that kept him from getting too close. Hiding behind a wall of unforgiveness is a lonely experience.

## Forgiveness Is Not Erasure

The modern idea of forgiveness is to approach an offense with a large eraser and wipe it off the books. God has never forgiven like this. For each offense, He demanded full payment. This is the reason for the cross. Beside every offense on our ledger is the blood of Christ, which has paid for our sins in full.

The Christian stands with a unique capacity for forgiveness because he or she can appropriate the forgiveness of the cross. God has forgiven us fully and completely. We, of all people, know what it is like to experience unconditional forgiveness. As a result, we can in turn forgive those around us. Think of it this way: *There is nothing that anyone can do to me (insult me, lie about me, annoy me, etc.) that can compare with what Christ has forgiven me for doing.* We gain a better perspective of others' offenses when we compare them to our sin of rebellion that Christ has completely forgiven. In Ephesians 4:32, Paul writes, *And be kind to one another, tender-hearted, forgiving each other, just as God in Christ also has forgiven you.*

Being offended or hurt by others is a frequent experience in life. The hurt comes from experiencing an offense—and then reliving it. In fact, the initial pain usually amounts to only a small fraction of the total hurt. The majority of the pain comes afterward as people dwell on the offense and their reaction to it. This can be avoided when they learn to deal with offenses rather than relive them countless times.

## God's Patience

The Lord is very patient. He knows some people would be overwhelmed if they concurrently experienced all the pain they have repressed and all of their own sinfulness. So He metes out new self-perceptions of wounds and sins as people grow in their ability to handle them. As they progress in the healing process, they typically remark, "I had no idea I had so much anger in me," or, "I've just seen a whole lot of hurt that I've never seen before." One man told me, "I don't know how many layers of hurt, anger, and sin I've gone through, but I'm glad I didn't see all of this at thc beginning! Every layer seems to be all I can take at that time. Sometimes I think God is harsh to let me go through all the pain, but then I realize He is really patient to let me feel only as much as I can take."

As you forgive people completely for all the wounds you see they have caused, you also need to realize that the wounds may be deeper and uglier than you perceive at that point. In the early stages, you can forgive all you see; then you see more, and forgive them for that, too. As the layers continue to be peeled back and more wounds are exposed, you can continue to completely forgive all you see. "I used to be surprised when I saw that the wounds were deeper than I originally thought," a lady told me, "but now, I'm not surprised any more. I expect to find more; but at every layer, I feel more freedom and more able to give and receive love."

Editor's note

At Rapha, we believe that small groups can provide a nurturing and powerful environment to help people deal with real-life problems such as depression, grief, fear, eating disorders, chemical dependency, codependency, and all kinds of other relational and emotional difficulties. The warmth, honesty, and understanding in those groups helps us understand why we feel and act the way we do. And with the encouragement of others, we can take definitive steps toward healing and health for ourselves and our relationships.

Not all groups, however, provide this kind of "greenhouse" for growth. Some only perpetuate the guilt and loneliness by giving quick and superficial solutions to the deep and often complex problems in our lives.

We urge you to find a group of people in your church, or in a church near you, where the members provide acceptance, love, honesty, and encouragement. Rapha has many different books, workbooks, leader's guides, and types of training so that people in these groups can be nurtured in the love and grace of God and focused on sound biblical principles to help them experience healing and growth.

To obtain a free list of the materials we have available, please write to us at:

Rapha, Inc.
8876 Gulf Freeway, Suite 340
Houston, TX 77017

# *About the Authors. . .*

**Robert S. McGee** is a professional counselor and lecturer who has helped thousands of people experience the love and acceptance of Jesus Christ. He is also the Founder and President of Rapha, a nationally recognized health care organization that provides in-house care with a Christ-centered perspective for adults and adolescents suffering with psychiatric and substance abuse problems. The truths presented in his book, *The Search for Significance*, form the foundational cornerstones that provide the balance of spiritual and clinical therapy in the Rapha Treatment Centers program.

He is also the author of *Discipline with Love* and co-author of several books, including *Rapha's 12-Step Program for Overcoming Chemical Dependency*, *Rapha's 12-Step Program for Overcoming Eating Disorders*, *Renew: Hope for Victims of Sexual Abuse*, and *Your Parents and You*.

**Pat Springle** is Senior Vice President, Church and Family Resources, for Rapha. He served on the staff of Campus Crusade for Christ for 18 years, 11 years as their Texas area director. Pat lives in Houston with his wife, Joyce, and his two children, Catherine and Taylor. He is the author or coauthor of several books, including *Rapha's 12–Step Program for Overcoming Codependency*, *Close Enough to Care*, and *Codependency: A Christian Perspective*.